PREVIOUSLY:

THE WORLD now lies divided not amongst political or geographic boundaries but amongst ***financial*** ones. Wealth is power, and that power rests with only a handful of **FAMILIES**.

The few who provide a service to their ruling Family are cared for and protected. They are **SERFS**.

All others are **WASTE**.

For almost four years, the **CONCLAVE WAR** has continued, with the **CARLYLE FAMILY** and their **LAZARUS**, **FOREVER CARLYLE**–a genetically engineered human weapon who, unbeknownst to her, was the seventh Forever created in a Carlyle lab–fighting against the **HOCK FAMILY** and its allies.

MALCOLM CARLYLE was poisoned by Hock and grew chronically ill. With the Head of Family incapacitated, his daughter **JOHANNA** rose to assume the position she'd coveted for years. Knowing that victory in the war required Forever's complete loyalty, Johanna went behind Malcolm's back and told Forever the truth that Malcolm had kept from her, including the existence of another Forever Carlyle, also known as **EIGHT**, a teen girl being trained and groomed to eventually take her place. Forever agreed to fight for Johanna, on the condition that Johanna let her have her free will and introduce her to their sister, Eight.

Late in the Year X +65, the Lazari from the **Armitage**, **Bittner**, and **Morray** Families joined Forever to fight the **Vassalovka** Lazarus, **THE ZMEY**–"The Dragon." The battle went poorly. Armitage's Lazarus was killed, and Morray's Lazarus–**JOACQUIM**, with whom Forever had formed a romantic attachment–was forced by his programming to betray Forever and Sonja Bittner, literally stabbing Forever in the back. Forever and Sonja barely escaped with their lives.

It is now early in the Year X +68. Enemies surround Carlyle on all sides; to the east, Hock; to the south, Morray; and now, preparing to advance through the Alaskan Expanse, Vassalovka. If something isn't done to turn the tide of war, Johanna knows Carlyle will be extinct by the end of the year.

Fortunately, she has a plan, one that is
Forever remaining at her sid

LAZARUS, VOLUME SIX: FRACTURE I

First printing. January 2020. Published by Image Comics, Inc. Office of publication: 2701 NW Vaugh St., Suite 780, Portland, OR 97210.

ISBN: 978-1-5343-0842-8

LAZARUS FRACTURED VOLUME SIX

written by **GREG RUCKA**

art by **MICHAEL LARK**
with **TYLER BOSS**

colors by **SANTI ARCAS**

letters by **JODI WYNNE**

cover by **MICHAEL LARK**

edited by **ALEJANDRO ARBONA**

publication design by **ERIC TRAUTMANN**

"artifact" design by **RICHARD HOWE**
and **ERIC TRAUTMANN**

Special thanks to **MIKHAIL KISELGOF, KIRA JOHNSON-HOWE, OZ DONALD, VERONICA HOWE,** and **GARETH-MICHAEL SKARKA.**

DRAMATIS PERSONAE

FAMILY: Carlyle
DOMAIN: Western United States (west coast of Alaska contested with Vassalovka); Western Canada; Northern Canada.
Allied with Morray, Carragher, Bittner. In conflict with Hock, Rausling, D'Souza, and Vassalovka.

JOHANNA CARLYLE
Acting Head of Family

MALCOLM CARLYLE
Patriarch of Family Carlyle; recovering from poisoning

CMDR. FOREVER CARLYLE
Family Carlyle Lazarus

DR. BETHANY CARLYLE
Daughter of Malcolm Carlyle

STEPHEN CARLYLE
Son of Malcolm Carlyle

EIGHT
Next-generation Lazarus

CARLYLE-AFFILIATED SERFS

ARTHUR COHN
Chief Family advisor

COMMANDING GENERAL DIEGO VALERI
Carlyle supreme military commander

GUNNERY SERGEANT MARISOL OCCAMPO
Dagger; combat instructor to Carlyle Lazarus

CORPORAL CASEY SOLOMON
Carlyle infantry soldier, hero of Duluth Campaign

DR. MICHAEL BARRETT
Former Waste; Lifted in X +64 for medical aptitude

DR. JAMES MANN
Deputy director of the Carlyle Family Lazarus program under Bethany Carlyle

SERÉ COOPER
Most popular anchor of Carlyle's entertainment/news programming

---

FAMILY: Morray
DOMAIN: Mexico and Central America, portions of the Caribbean.
Member of Carlyle Bloc. In conflict with D'Souza and Hock.

EDGAR MORRAY
Head of Family Morray

JOACQUIM MORRAY
Family Morray Lazarus

FAMILY: D'Souza
DOMAIN: Portugal, Spain, and the Southern Cone region of South America.
Member of Carlyle bloc. In conflict with Hock and Rausling.

ZEFERINO CARDOSO
D'Souza Family Lazarus

MILY: Vassalovka
MAIN: Eastern Europe,
st-Soviet states throughout
thern Asia, and Svalbard and the
tic Ocean extending through
stern Alaska.
conflict with Carlyle bloc.

THE ZMEY
Family Vassalovka Lazarus

MILY: Armitage
MAIN: United Kingdom of
eat Britain and Ireland-
de-One.
t of the Carlyle bloc.
conflict with Rausling and
Souza.

HRH THE DUKE OF LANCASTER EDWARD ARMITAGE
Head of Family Armitage

SIR THOMAS HUSTON
Family Armitage Lazarus
KIA X +65

SIR THOMAS HUSTON
Next iteration of Family Armitage Lazarus

MILY: Bittner
MAIN: Canada (former
vinces of Ontario, Quebec,
wfoundland & Labrador);
rthern Europe/North Atlantic
itzerland, Scandinavia),
rmany.
mber of Carlyle bloc.
conflict with Hock and
usling.

SEVARA BITTNER
Head of Family Bittner

SONJA BITTNER
Family Bittner Lazarus

MILY: Hock
MAIN: Former United States,
st of the Mississippi; portions
the Caribbean; portions of
utheastern Canada.
ied with Vassalovka,
usling, and D'Souza.
conflict with Armitage,
rlyle, Bittner, Morray.

DR. JAKOB HOCK
Head of Family; bitter enemy of Malcolm Carlyle

MILY: Rausling
MAIN: Austria, Poland, portions
Central Europe, between Bittner-
ntrolled Western Europe and
ssalovka-controlled
ssia; Greece, excluding Meyers-
simi held Crete and Cyprus.
MILY ELIMINATED BY CARLYLE
OC.

LUKA RAUSLING
Head of Family Rausling

CAPTAIN CRISTOF MUELLER
Family Rausling Lazarus

MICHAEL LARK

FRACTURE I

CHAPTER ONE

February, X +68
Far North Sub-Dominion – Nunavut – Baker Lake
Family: Carlyle
Lesser House: Aklaq
Population [Serf]: Data Unavailable
Population [Waste]: Data Unavailable
BLUE WOLF, GORGON. SET READY, OVER.
GORGON, BLUE WOLF. FIRST TEAM AT READY, OVER.

GORGON, ALL TEAMS, STAND BY...

...WE HAVE **EYES** ON ARRIVAL.

SNAKEBITE, VERIFY TARGET.
ACQUIRING.
4X

GOOD **IMAGE**, GOING FOR **CAPTURE.**
TRANSMITTING...
RUNNING FACIAL RECOG

MATCH
...AAAND **CONFIRMATION.** IT'S HER...
FACIAL RECOG: MATCH: 99.712%
SUB: KOPYLOV, TATIANA_

REPEAT, TARGET CONFIRMED.

SPYGLASS, GORGON...

...TAG THE TARGETS.

SPYGLASS, GORGON, ACQUIRING...

...STAND BY.

ACQUIRING.

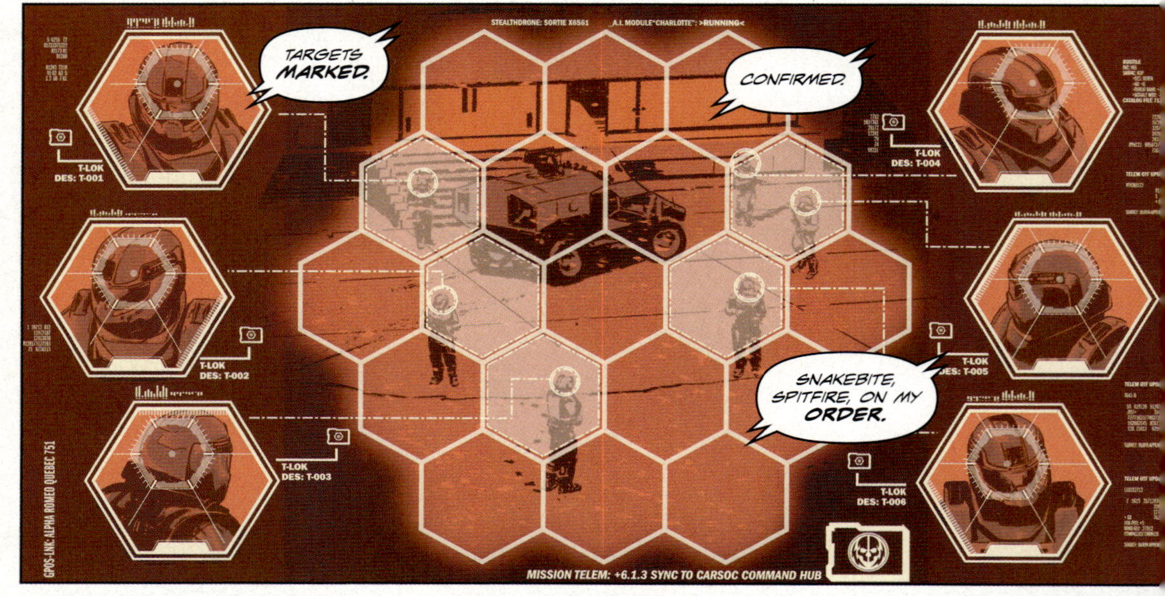
STEALTHDRONE: SORTIE X6561
A.I. MODULE "CHARLOTTE": >RUNNING<
TARGETS MARKED.
CONFIRMED.
T-LOK DES: T-001
T-LOK DES: T-002
T-LOK DES: T-003
T-LOK DES: T-004
T-LOK DES: T-005
T-LOK DES: T-006
SNAKEBITE, SPITFIRE, ON MY ORDER.
GPOS-LNK: ALPHA ROMEO QUEBEC 751
MISSION TELEM: +6.1.3 SYNC TO CARSOC COMMAND HUB

EXECUTE.

TARGETS DOWN.

...MARK.

CARLYLE

CARLYLE

TANGO DOWN.
I'LL POP THE LOCKS, YOU GET THE GOODIES.

GOVERNOR AKLAQ?
WH...

...YOU'RE NOT ONE OF RUDY'S TRAITORS.

NO, MA'AM.
WE'RE HERE TO TAKE BACK WHAT YOUR BROTHE STOLE.
GORGON, SPITFIRE. PACKAGE IS SECURE.
NICE JOB. STAND BY TO DELIVER.

--TO TALK TO HIM...

...I WANT HIS ASSURANCE.
I SPEAK FOR HIM, MISTER AKLAQ.
BUT YOU'RE NOT HIM, MISS KOPYLOV, AND HE'S WHO I'M DEALING WITH.

I TALK TO YOUR FATHER OR NO DEAL.

VERY WELL...

...YOU'LL FIND HE'S BEEN LISTENING ALL ALONG.

YOU WANT MY ASSURANCE, MISTER AKLAQ?
MY WORD IS THE BEST YOU WILL GET.

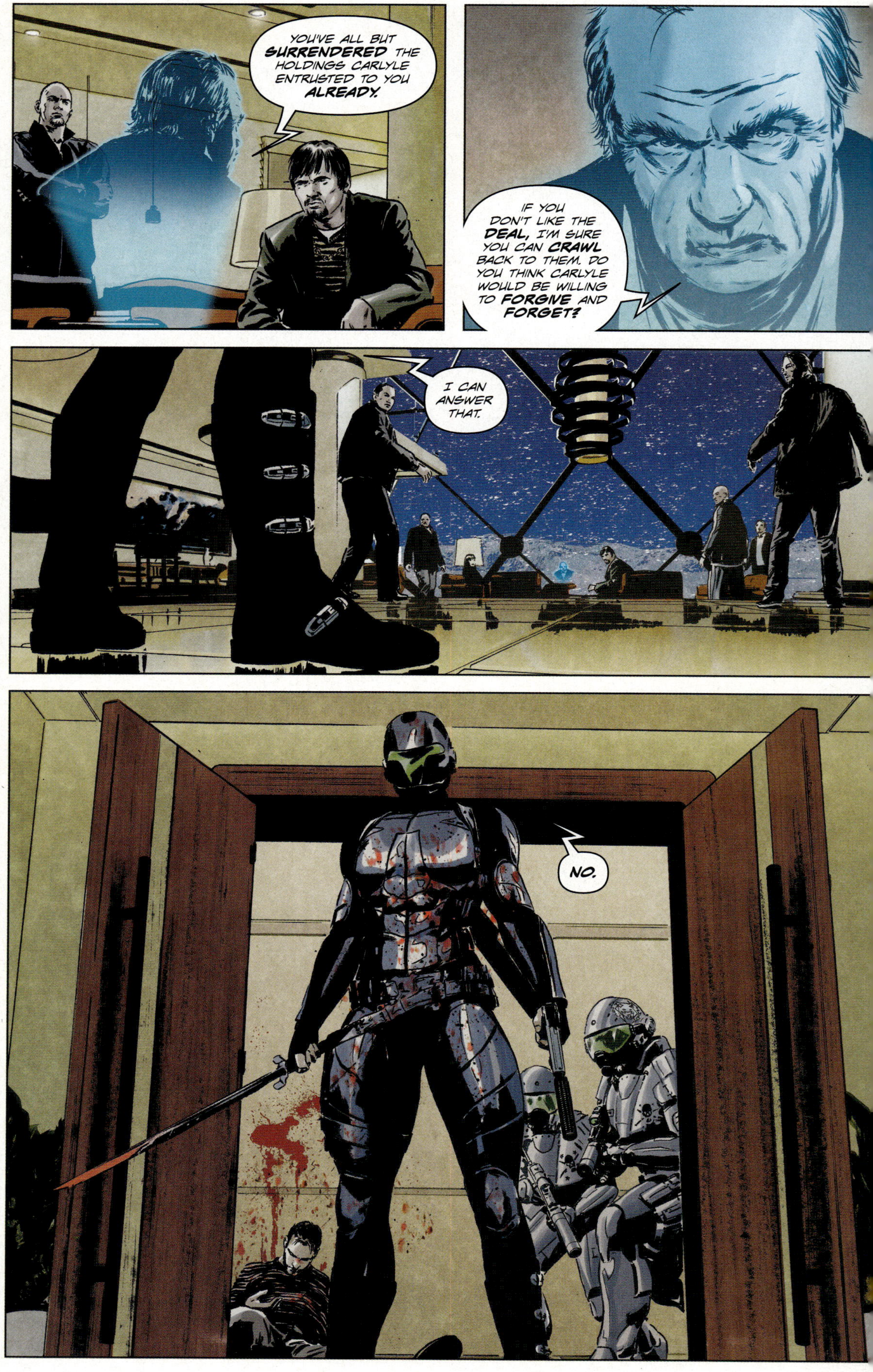

YOU'VE ALL BUT **SURRENDERED** THE HOLDINGS CARLYLE ENTRUSTED TO YOU **ALREADY.**

IF YOU DON'T LIKE THE **DEAL,** I'M SURE YOU CAN **CRAWL** BACK TO THEM. DO YOU THINK CARLYLE WOULD BE WILLING TO **FORGIVE** AND **FORGET?**

I CAN ANSWER THAT.

NO.

RUDY AKLAQ, I ARREST YOU FOR **HIGH TREASON** AGAINST MY FAMILY.

N-**NO** WAI--

SHUT UP, YOU TRAITOROUS COCKFUCK.
NHHN--

SHE MOVES, **KILL** HER.
SHE ENDS THE TRANSMISSION TO HER FATHER, **KILL** HER.
ROGER THAT.

YOU CAN COME IN.

MIRANDA, PLEASE--

WOW, YOU'RE JUST GETTING EVERYTHING WRONG TONIGHT, AREN'T YOU, RUDY?

MISS CARLYLE-- JOHANNA-- IT'S NOT WH--

HE SAYS ANOTHER WORD WITHOUT MY PERMISSION, BREAK HIS FUCKING JAW, PLEASE.
WITH PLEASURE.

YOU MUST BE TATIANA. I'M JOHANNA CARLYLE.
NO, PLEASE, DON'T HANG UP. I WANT YOU AND YOUR FATHER BOTH TO SEE THIS NEXT PART.

GOVERNOR? IF YOU'D LIKE TO JOIN US?

MIRANDA... MIRANDA, PLEASE--

NHRRHH HNRRNN...
YOU WERE TOLD WHAT WOULD HAPPEN IF YOU SPOKE WITHOUT PERMISSION.

IF YOU AND YOUR FATHER WILL INDULGE ME FOR A MOMENT, TATIANA...
...HAVE TO TAKE CARE OF SOME HOUSEKEEPING, FIRST.

SO, LET'S SEE, WHERE DO WE START, RUDY?
AKLAQ IS A LESSER HOUSE, RAISED BY CARLYLE-- BY MY FATHER-- TO A POSITION OF TRUST AND HONOR.
YOUR FAMILY'S DUTY WAS SIMPLE BUT VITAL: TO ADMINISTER THE FAR NORTH SUB-DOMINION IN MY FAMILY'S NAME.

YOU WERE TO CARE FOR OUR PEOPLE. YOU WERE TO DEFEND THE TERRITORY. YOU WERE TO FIGHT OUR ENEMIES.

OH, AND YOU WERE TO FOLLOW THE HEAD OF YOUR FAMILY, YOUR SISTER, WHO WAS NAMED GOVERNOR BY MY FATHER, NO LESS.

INSTEAD, YOU LAUNCHED A LITTLE COUP AND OPENED OUR LANDS TO VASSALOVKA.
VASSALOVKA TROOPS, RUDY...

...ON CARLYLE SOIL.

THAT'S HIGH FUCKING TREASON, RUDY.
I SHOULD LET MY SISTER CUT OFF YOUR BALLS AND MAKE YOU EAT THEM.

BUT I'M NOT GOING TO DO THAT.
INSTEAD, I'M GOING TO LET YOUR SISTER PASS SENTENCE.

SHE IS THE RIGHTFUL GOVERNOR, AFTER ALL.
I'M SURE YOU CAN EXPECT HER TO SHOW YOU THE SAME MERCY YOU SHOWED HER.

YOU'RE MY FAMILY, RUDY...
...YOU'RE MY BROTHER...

...AND YOU USED ME... YOU ABUSED ME...YOU'D HAVE KILLED ME...

...AND PERHAPS I COULD FORGIVE YOU ALL OF THAT, BUT YOU BETRAYED NOT JUST OUR NAME BUT THE TRUST CARLYLE PLACED IN US.

AS THE APPOINTED GOVERNOR, IN THE NAME OF THE CARLYLE FAMILY, I FIND YOU, RUDY AKLAQ, GUILTY OF THE CRIME OF HIGH TREASON.
MRRNRR EEZ RRNDD!
THE PENALTY IS DEATH.

NNRRRR!
MRRNRR EEEZ--

--EEZ MRRNR UH GGE EEZ--

IF THAT LITTLE DISPLAY OF CARLYLE JUSTICE IS OVER...

...MY DAUGHTER WILL NOW BE TAKING HER LEAVE.

YOUR DAUGHTER--
--YOUR ADOPTED, ONLY CHILD, IN FACT--
--ISN'T GOING ANYWHERE...

...AT LEAST, NOT **YET.**
TATIANA! YOU WILL SAY **NOTHING,** YOU WILL GIVE THEM **NOTHING!**

A SINGLE **HARM** COMES TO MY DAUGHTER, I WILL UNLEASH **HELL** ON CARLYLE!
I WILL **DESTROY** YOUR FAMILY MYSELF, NOT IN VASSALOVKA'S NAME--

--BUT IN MY **OWN,** I SHALL--

MY FATHER WON'T EVER SHUT **UP,** EITHER.
NOW, THEN, TATIANA...

...LET'S TALK ABOUT HOW CARLYLE CAN HELP **YOU...**
...AND HOW **YOU** AND YOUR FATHER CAN HELP **CARLYLE...**

MY FATHER IS A **REASONABLE** MAN AND YOUR PROPOSAL IS A REASONABLE **ONE.**

YOU'LL HEAR FROM US BY TOMORROW.
I'LL BE WAITING.

PREP FOR DEPARTURE.

SO FAR, SO GOOD.

Mhm.
UH-OH, I KNOW THAT NOISE.
WHAT'S WRONG?

NOTHING.
YOU ARE SO FULL OF SHIT.
THIS WENT EXACTLY AS WE'D HOPED! MY GOD, IT FEELS LIKE IT'S BEEN YEARS SINCE SOMETHING'S GONE ACCORDING TO PLAN!
THIS WAS THE HARD PART. HANDLING D'SOUZA WILL BE EASY COMPARED TO THIS.

WE MIGHT ACTUALLY, Y'KNOW, SURVIVE THIS WAR, OR EVEN--GOD FORBID!--WIN IT!

BIG "IF," JO.
MY FAITH IN YOU REMAINS UNSHAKABLE.

HEY. NO SECRETS BETWEEN US, THAT WAS THE DEAL, REMEMBER?
TALK TO ME, FOREVER.

WHEN DO I GET TO MEET HER, JO?
IT'S BEEN TWO YEARS, I'VE BEEN PATIENT, BUT...

I'M WORKING ON IT.
THAT'S WHAT YOU ALWAYS SAY.

CAN WE NOT TALK ABOUT THIS NOW?
Y'KNOW, IN THE MIDDLE OF A FROZEN LAKE WITH ALL OF DAGGER ALPHA IN EARSHOT?

THEY CAN'T HEAR US.
YOU PROMISED, JO. I'VE DONE EVERYTHING YOU'VE ASKED.

YOU PROMISED.

AND I'VE DONE EVERYTHING ELSE I PROMISED, HAVEN'T I?
I'VE BEEN HONEST WITH YOU AT EVERY TURN.

I GOT DOCTOR BARRETT TO GET YOU CLEAN OF JAMES AND BETH'S DRUGS, THEY CAN'T CONTROL YOU ANYMORE.
YOU CAN THINK FOR YOURSELF, NOW, YOU DON'T HAVE TO DO WHAT YOU'RE TOLD.

THIS IS HARDER THAN THAT. YOU KNOW WHAT THE SECURITY AT SEQUOIA IS LIKE.
THEY WATCH HER TWENTY-FOUR-SEVEN, JUST LIKE YOU WERE. AND SHE'S STILL A KID, FOREVER...

...WHAT HAPPENS IF SHE TELLS SOMEONE SHE KNOWS ABOUT YOU?
HAVE YOU EVEN THOUGHT ABOUT THAT?

I'LL MAKE IT HAPPEN. I JUST NEED TIME.
AND I NEED YOU TO KEEP TRUSTING ME.

I DO.

uthern Sierra Nevadas
cility: Compound Sequoia
mily: Carlyle
INCREASE GRADE SEVEN PERCENT, DECREASE OH-TWO BY HALF...

opulation [Family]: 2 (2 permanent)
opulation [Serf]: 103
...GOOD... INCREASE PACE ANOTHER TEN PERCENT.
SORRY, DID YOU SAY TEN PERCENT?
SERVER STACK

DID I STUTTER?
NO, MA'AM, DOCTOR CARLYLE...

...ACCELERATING TO FIFTY-SEVEN-POINT-FIVE KILOMETERS PER HOUR.
MAKE IT A ROUND SIXTY...

...LET'S SEE IF SHE CAN TAKE IT.

PACE
58.213 KMPH
1:20:09.1
TIME ELAPSED
+16.4
PULM. STRESS MARKERS

PACE
59.01 KMPH
1:21:29.3
TIME ELAPSED
+17.064
PULM. STRESS MARKERS

NHN

PACE
60.0512 KMPH
1:23:49.9
TIME ELAPSED
+28.91
PULM. STRESS MARKERS

NHHH--

KRNNCH

STAY ON POST! STAY ON YOUR POSTS!

MOVE! FUCKING MOVE!
SECTION

JESUS FUCK.

FOREVER, HOLD ON--
DON'T TOUCH HER...

...LEAVE HER ALONE.

CLEAR THE ROOM!
EVE...
...BABY...

DAMMIT, MARISOL! I SAID DON'T TOUCH HER...

...WE'RE TIMING HER RECOVERY.

HKK KNHN...
K-K-G-G...

...G-GO AWAY...

...J-JUST *KAF* GO A-A-AWAY...
GET UP.
O₂ FLOW 96.6%

I SAID, GET UP.
SIX FRACTURED RIBS, MULTIPLE CONTUSIONS, SHATTERED PELVIS, SOFT-TISSUE DAMAGE, INTERNAL HEMORRHAGE...

...FULL RECOVERY SHOULD TAKE YOU LESS THAN A MINUTE, FOREVER.

GET UP!
WHY ARE YOU STILL ON THE GROUND, YOUNG LADY?

BECAUSE...

...IT FUCKING HURTS!

DON'T YOU EVER RAISE YOUR VOICE AT ME AGAIN.

BETHANY!
DON'T FUCKING TALK TO ME, JAMES...

...I'M THE ONLY ONE AROUND HERE WHO SEEMS TO CARE ANYMORE...

SHE DOES IT ON **PURPOSE.**
SHE HURTS ME ON **PURPOSE,** MARISOL.

SHE'S MY **SISTER.**

WHY?

I DON'T KNOW, KIDDO.

uget Sound – The Center
amily: Carlyle

IT WAS **STUPID** AND **DANGEROUS** AND SHE SHOULD **NEVER** HAVE DONE IT.

opulation [Family]: 4 (3 permanent)

WHICH IS WHY YOU WERE KEPT **OUT** OF THE LOOP, I SUSPECT, ADMIRAL.

I'M HER CHIEF OF INTELLIGENCE! I'VE GOT **ENOUGH** SECRETS TO FERRET OUT WITHOUT WORRYING ABOUT WHAT SHE'S HIDING FROM ME AS WELL, ARTHUR!

WITH GOOD REASON.
THE HEAD OF FAMILY TRAVELING INTO A HOSTILE THEATER?
VASSALOVKA COULD'VE CAPTURED OR KILLED YOU, MISS CARLYLE.

IF IT HAD GONE WRONG WE'D ALL BE CHOKING ON HOCK'S HAPPY PILLS RIGHT NOW.

I WAS AWARE OF THE RISKS WHEN I UNDERTOOK THE OPERATION, ADMIRAL.
BUT I ALSO KNEW THOSE RISKS WEREN'T NEARLY AS GREAT AS YOU IMAGINED THEM TO BE.
OH, DID YOU? AND HOW DID YOU KNOW THAT?

BECAUSE MY SISTER WAS WITH ME.

GENERAL VALERI WILL CONFERENCE IN SHORTLY.
IN THE MEANTIME, WE SHOULD GET STARTED...

...ADMIRAL SANGER, IF YOU'LL BRIEF US ON THE SITUATION WITH THE D'SOUZA FAMILY, PLEASE...

FATHER?

FOREVER. HELLO.
I THOUGHT YOU WERE ALREADY ON YOUR WAY.

NOT UNTIL NIGHTFALL.
I'D WISH YOU LUCK, BUT WE BOTH KNOW HOW OUR FAMILY'S LUCK HAS GONE THE LAST FEW YEARS.

YESTERDAY'S ADVENTURE IN THE FROZEN NORTH NOTWITHSTANDING, OF COURSE.
OF COURSE.

YOU'RE UP FOR WHAT YOU NEED TO DO NEXT?
YES.
YES, I AM.

I WORRY ABOUT YOU, YOU KNOW.
WE ASK SO MUCH OF YOU.

BE SAFE, FOREVER.

IT'S JAMES...

...MAY I COME IN?
...BETHANY? MAY I COME IN...?

BETH?
RIGHT HERE...

...HAVE A DRINK.
OR A SMOKE.

YOU WANT A SMOKE, JAMES?
OR DO YOU WANT SOMETHING ELSE?

I WANTED... WE NEED TO TALK.

I DON'T WANT TO TALK. I'M OFF THE CLOCK.
THIS IS ME TIME.
ME ME ME ME ME TIME.

UNLESS YOU WANT TO MAKE IT US TIME.
WE USED TO FUCK QUITE A LOT, DIDN'T WE, JAMES?
BACK IN THE DAY.

LIKE RRRABBITS.

SHOULD I ASK HOW HIGH YOU ARE?

YOU SHOULD NOT.
BUT SINCE YOU JUST DID WHILE PRETENDING NOT TO, THE ANSWER IS:
NOT NEARLY ENOUGH.

WE NEED TO TALK ABOUT WHAT HAPPENED TODAY--
--WE NEED TO TALK ABOUT FOREVER.
NO, WE DEFINITELY DON'T.

DO WE? HICH ONE? MEAN, YOU'VE GOT EIGHT O CHOOSE FROM.
FUCK, WE'RE ALREADY IN GESTATION ON THE NINTH, YOU WANT TO TALK ABOUT HER?
WHAT YOU DID TODAY DURING THE RUN TEST WAS CRUEL--

WHAT DO YOU KNOW ABOUT CRUEL?

YOU, OF ALL PEOPLE.
YOU FUCKING LECTURE ME ABOUT CRUEL.
BETH, THAT'S NOT--

YOU WERE THERE.
YOU WERE THERE.

EVERY TIME, YOU WERE THERE.
WHEN I HAD TO PULL THE PLUG ON THEM. NOT YOU.
WHEN I HAD TO KILL THEM.

BECAUSE THEY WEREN'T RIGHT...
BETH, I'M SORRY. I DIDN'T THINK, I'M SORRY.
...AND NOW...

...AND NOW, JAMES...
SHH, SHH, BETH...

...I'M NOT SMART ENOUGH...
...IT'S ALL RIGHT...
...I'LL NEVER BE AS SMART AS SHE WAS...

...MOM WOULD KNOW WHAT TO DO.

LOAD AND PROJECT, TELOMERE TRACK, MALCOLM CARLYLE.
GIVE ME THE LAST THREE YEARS.
BA-DEET

ANALYSIS:
_MALCOLM_LONGEV SEQUENCE
ETECTED! ALERT! ERRORS DETECTED!

The Atlantic Ocean, 5°11’26” N, 50°09’50” W
aunch Platform Relâmpago
amily: D’Souza

THERE SHE IS.

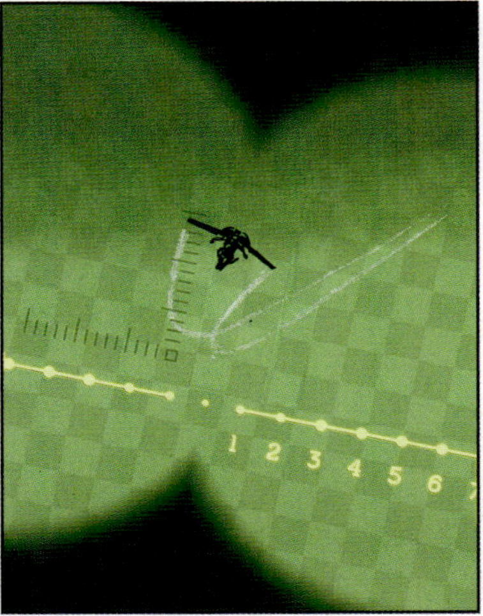
1 2 3 4 5 6

FOREVER.

ZEFERINO.

D'SOUZA WELCOMES YOU.
AND CARLYLE APPRECIATES D'SOUZA'S HOSPITALITY...

...FOR AS LONG AS IT MAY LAST.

IT WILL LAST UNTIL D'SOUZA HAS WHAT IT WANTS, OF COURSE.

AT THE END OF THE DAY, FOREVER, IT IS ABOUT ONE THING AND ONE THING ALONE, NO MATTER THE FAMILY...

...SURVIVAL.

HEY, BABY.
SHALL WE DANCE?

CARLYLE
ODERINT DUM METUANT

MICHAEL LARK AND ERIC TRAUTMANN

FRACTURE

CHAPTER TWO

The Atlantic Ocean,
5°11'26" N, 50°09'50" W
Launch Platform *Relâmpago*
JUST **KILL** HER.

Family: D'Souza
NOT YET.
I LIKED YOU BETTER WITH **LONG** HAIR, FOREVER...

...IT MADE YOU LOOK **PRETTY.**
OHH, DON'T BE LIKE **THAT...**

...I THOUGHT YOU **LOVED** ME ONCE, **BABY.**
HNNN

STOP FUCKING AROUND, JUST TAKE HER HEAD AND BE DONE WITH IT!
NOT--

--YET.
Y'KNOW, IT'S FUNNY...

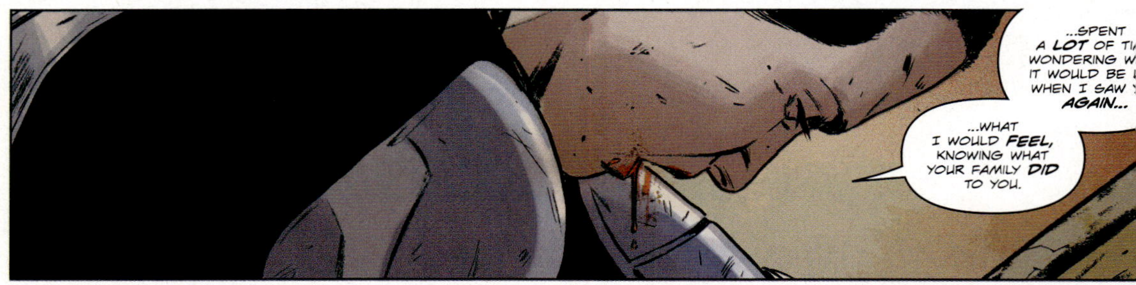
...SPENT A LOT OF TI
WONDERING W
IT WOULD BE
WHEN I SAW
AGAIN...
...WHAT I WOULD FEEL, KNOWING WHAT YOUR FAMILY DID TO YOU.

WHAT YOU WOULD FEEL, FOREVER?

NNNHH!
KRIK
PAIN, OF COURSE.

A LOT OF PAIN.
MEU DEUS, JOACQUIM...
GGHNNN

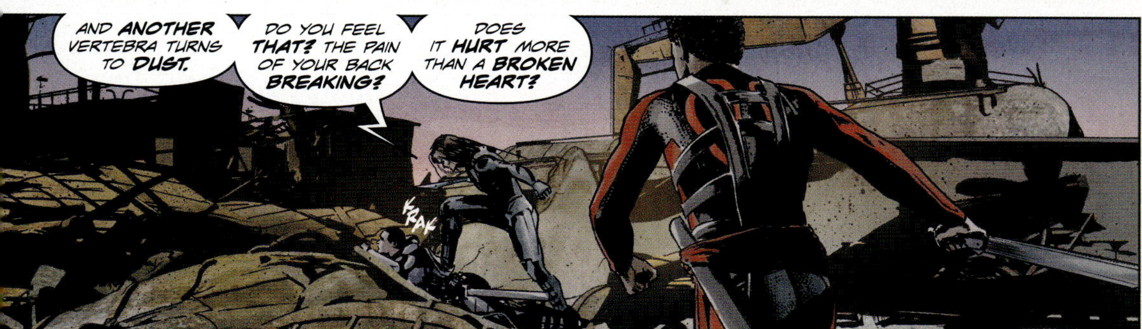
AND ANOTHER VERTEBRA TURNS TO DUST.
DO YOU FEEL THAT? THE PAIN OF YOUR BACK BREAKING?
DOES IT HURT MORE THAN A BROKEN HEART?
KRAK

KKRRK
NHNNN HNH HUH...
JOACQUIM...

YES, DARLING?
...YOU SHOULD'VE LISTENED TO--

--ZEFERINO!

WHOEVER IS RUNNING THAT SHELL, YOU'RE NOT JOACQUIM.

YOU THOUGHT I'D GO ALL WEAK-KNEED AT THE SIGHT OF WHAT'S BECOME OF HIM?
PLEASE.

OOOH, YOU BROKE MY BACK!
DID YOU FORGET WHO CARLYLE IS? DID YOU FORGET WHAT WE'RE CAPABLE OF?
TWO LITTLE BOYS, TRYING TO BE A LAZARUS...

...I AM THE LAZARUS.

YOU GET ONE CHANCE.
THROW DOWN YOUR WEAPONS, SURRENDER YOURSELVES AND YOUR FAMILIES TO CARLYLE UNCONDITIONALLY...
...OR I KILL YOU BOTH HERE.

THEN I KILL EVERY LAST MEMBER OF YOUR FAMILIES.
SISTERS AND FATHERS. BROTHERS AND MOTHERS.
ALL OF THEM DIE ON MY SWORD.

YOU WILL BE SCREAMING FOR MERCY BEFORE THE END.

THIS IS ONLY BUSINESS, FOREVER.
CARLYLE'S TIME IS PAST.
OF COURSE IT'S BUSINESS, ZEFERINO...

...THAT'S WHY IT'S PERSONAL.

FLANK HER--

--RNNAANNN

YOUR TEAMWORK--

--SUCKS ASS.

LOOK AT YOU TWO.
PATHETIC.

YOU THINK YOU'RE ON TOP, BUT INSTEAD YOU'RE CLUMSY AND SLOW.

YOU THINK YOU'RE CLEVER AND SUBTLE, BUT YOU'RE BEHIND THE CURVE AND OUT OF YOUR DEPTH.

JUST LIKE YOUR FAMILIES.

FUCK--

--YOU CU--

--NT YO--

--U--

MERDA...

JOACQUIM!
COME ON!

GAAAAHH!

WHERE IS SHE?
HIDING.

SHE'S HIDING.

I'LL HEAD--
NO. DON'T SPLIT UP.
THAT'S WHAT SHE WANTS.

WE STAY TOGETHER.

T.1
EL BLANCO PRINCIPAL:
BUSCANDO

JOACQUIM!

MOVE!

LITTLE BITCH...

"...SHE'S **PLAYING** WITH US."
T-1

A_001
3X
BLANCO PRINCIPAL
QUIRIDO

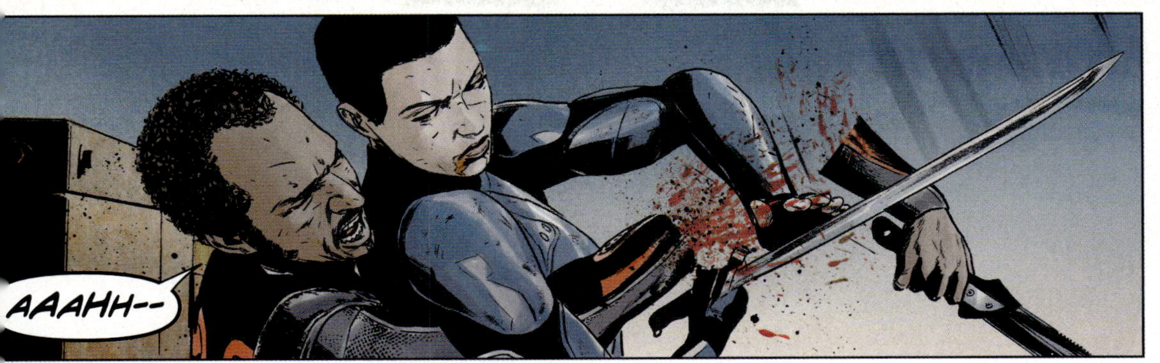
AAAHH--

5X
EL BLANCO PRINCIPAL:
ADQUIRIDO

YOU'RE RIGHT. I'M NOT HIM.
HE'S DEAD.

DO YOU KNOW WHY WE HAD TO DELETE JOACQUIM, FOREVER?
BECAUSE YOU'RE SICK FUCKS.

BECAUSE HE BROKE THE FIRST RULE. FAMILY ABOVE ALL.
AND HE FORGOT THAT...
...AND PUT YOU ABOVE FAMILY.

JUST...
...FINISH IT.

MORRAY THANKS YOU FOR DISPOSING OF ZEFERINO.
D'SOUZA WILL BE EASIER TO DEAL WITH NOW THAT HE'S GONE.

GHU

UNNGGG

GAAA!

AAAA
AAAAAA--

--AAAAA FUCK YOU FUCK--

--YOU FUCKYOU FUCKYOU FUC--

--K YOU!

_E_TRANS_
ERROR

SIGNAL
_LOSS_REACQUIR_
->SKSSS<-_ING__
ERROR_
_INIT_FAI_
->SKSSS<-L...

...FOREVER...

...FOREVER...

...PLEASE...

...IF YOU...
...IF YOU EVER...

...PLEASE...

UHN

HHNH

HNNGH

Southern Sierra Nevadas
Facility: Compound Sequoia
Family: Carlyle

COMBAT TELEMETRY
BASELINES NORMAL.
GOOD. GET AN ETA ON TRANSPORT, I WANT TO SEE HER AS SOON AS SHE'S BACK. FULL SUITE DIAGNOSTICS, AND I WANT AN IPS PUSH TO--

I'M AFRAID COMMANDER CARLYLE IS NEEDED ELSEWHERE, DOCTOR.
I BEG YOUR PARDON?
BY YOUR SISTER'S ORDER.

MY SISTER DOESN'T RUN THE LAZARUS PROGRAM, ADMIRAL SANGER.
IT'S MY RESPONSIBILITY TO MAKE CERTAIN FOREVER IS OPERATING AT PEAK--
THEN YOU NEED TO TAKE THE MATTER UP WITH HER--
--ADMIRAL SANGER, MA'AM. WE'RE READY...
REEN
BASELINE

...CORRECT, BOTH OF THEM. GORGON-ACTUAL ON HER WAY BACK NOW...

STREAMING

I'LL START ON THE TELEMETRY DATA RIGHT AWAY.
I CAN HAVE AN ANALYSIS ON YOUR DESK IN AN HOUR.
SERVER Q-76J

WHAT'S THE FUCKING POINT?
SYSTEM LOAD
STREAMING

Southwest Domain
Lone Star Sub-Dominion

Family: Carlyle

Facility: CAIR Base Leah
Population [Serf]: 2,101

COMMANDER.
LET ME HELP.

THANKS, MIKE.

IT LOOKED BAD. FROM THE TELEMETRY, I MEAN.
YEAH.

YEAH, IT WAS.

I'VE GOT YOUR iPS PUSH, HAT'LL HELP THE REGEN.
YOU WANT ANYTHING FOR THE PAIN?
YOU ALWAYS ASK...
WELL, IT'S KINDA MY JOB, COMMANDER.

...YOU'RE THE ONLY ONE WHO EVER ASKS...

...ATTACK LAUNCHED MOMENTS AGO BY LAND, SEA, AND AIR...

...AS CARLYLE FORCES BEGAN AN ALL-OUT ASSAULT ON THE MORRAY DOMAIN.
BOMBARDMENTS TARGETING INFRASTRUCTURE AS WELL AS COMMUNICATIONS AND MANUFACTURING ARE SAID TO BE ONGOING.
MANDATORY EVACUATIONS ARE IN EFFECT FOR AREAS OF THE LONE STAR, SOUTHWEST, AND PACIFIC SUB-DOMINIONS IN ANTICIPATION OF AN ENEMY COUNTER-OFFENSIVE.
NEWSBRIEF
NEWS ALERT
EVACUATION IS PRECAUTIONARY, TO AVOID CASUALTIES IN THE EVENT OF A MORRAY COUNTERSTRIKE.
SEAN CARLTON
SNR. ANCHOR
OPERATION SISYPHUS
LIVE
ERATION: SISYPHUS" • CAIR SORTIES ONGOING •
AUTIONARY EVACUATION ORDERED •
CEEtv

VIEWERS ARE ADVISED TO MONITOR THEIR LOCAL POST BROADCASTS--
FOR FUCK'S SAKE, MUTE ALREADY.
TASK LIST
KNOW YOUR EVAC ROUTE
RE FOR POSSIBLE MORRAY COUNTER ATTAC

LIGHTS OFF.

OCCAMPO.
GET ME THE DUTY OFFICER.
CALL: RUNNING
C11-524-7182 X 81
VOX ONLY
[DUTY OFFICER]
AT ONCE, SERGEANT.

RAFFETTO. WHAT CAN I DO FOR YOU, GUNNY?
HEY, JAMES, YOU GOT ANYTHING **OUTSIDE** OF KAPPA RIGHT NOW?
ASIDE FROM THE FOOT PATROL, YOU MEAN?

THAT'S WHAT I MEAN, YEAH.
CHECKING.
HAD A **WILDLIFE** TRIGGER AT TWENTY-THREE-SEVENTEEN.
THERMAL REGISTERED IT AS A **BEAR.**

WANT ME TO DISPATCH **SWEEPERS?**
NO, THANKS, JAMES.
A BEAR, HUH? MAYBE I'LL GO TAKE A **LOOK.**
COMMON AMERICAN BLACK BEAR, THERE'S A FAIR NUMBER OF THEM ABOUT THIS TIME OF YEAR.

CALL: RUNNING
C11-524-7182 X 81
VOX ONLY
[GUARD STATION: A-5]
[DUTY OFFICER]
"COMMON BLACK BEAR."

PPA

OH, IT'S YOU, GUNNY.
APOLOGIES.
NOTHING TO APOLOGIZE FOR, DORÉ.

JUST GOING FOR A LITTLE ***WALK.***
BACK IN A BIT.

FOREVER?

EVE?
I CAN'T DO IT, MARISOL.

WHY CAN'T I DO IT?

OH, BABY.
OH, GOD, EVE.

WHY CAN'T I DIE?

WHY DON'T I DIE?
EVE, SHH, SHH...

...IT'S OKAY, BABY, I'M HERE...
NO MATTER WHAT I DO...

...I CAN'T DIE...
...I KNOW, BABY. IT'S OKAY, I'M HERE, I WON'T LEAVE YOU...

...I'LL NEVER LEAVE YOU...

Puget Sound
Facility: The Center
Family: Carlyle
...SANGER REPORTS THAT FOREVER AND DAGGER ALPHA SUCCESSFULLY DESTROYED MORRAY'S MAIN REMOTE CONTROL HUB...

Population [Family]: 2
...IT'S THROWN THE MECHANIZED AND DRONE UNITS INTO DISARRAY.
VALERI IS PRESSING THE ADVANTAGE.
IT'LL GET UGLY WHEN THEY REACH MEXICO CITY.

JO'S ORDERED VALERI NOT TO TRY TO TAKE THE CITY.
STRATEGY IS TO ISOLATE MORRAY'S FORCES, THEN COLLAPSE AROUND THE POCKETS OF RESISTANCE.

INTERESTING. I'D BE CURIOUS TO KNOW IF SHE CAME UP WITH THAT STRATEGY HERSELF OR IF SHE HAD HELP.
FROM FOREVER, YOU MEAN?

THEY HAVE BE SPENDING LOT OF T TOGETHE
THEY SEEM TO HAV GROWN QUIT CLOSE.

SOMETHING TO BE THANKFUL FOR, MALCOLM.
YOU WON'T STAY FOR ANOTHER DRINK?

HAVE TO GET BACK TO VANCOUVER TONIGHT. I'LL BE BACK DOWN BY THE END OF THE WEEK.
THEN I'LL WISH YOU GOOD NIGHT AND SAFE TRAVELS, ARTHUR.
MY LOVE TO YOUR FAMILY.

NOK NOK NOK

GOOD EVENING, HAILEY.

I WAS... WONDERING IF SHE MIGHT BE WILLING TO SEE ME?
GOOD EVENING, SIR.
WHY DON'T YOU COME IN AND TAKE A **SEAT...**

...I'LL GO AND TELL HER YOU'RE **HERE.**
THANK YOU.

DOCTOR? YOUR **HUSBAND** IS HERE TO SEE YOU...

I'M SORRY, MISTER CARLYLE...

...I'M AFRAID SHE DOESN'T WISH TO SEE YOU RIGHT NOW.

...
I UNDERSTAND.
THANK YOU, HAILEY.

PLEASE GIVE HER MY LOVE.

I ALWAYS DO, SIR.
GOOD NIGHT, SIR.

CAIR One
In transit over Cascadia Sub-Dominion
...FIGHTING AMONGST THE EASTERN AVTORITETS IN VASSALOVKA TERRITORY SEEN IN THE SMUGGLED FOOTAGE...

...LEADING TO FURTHER SPECULATION THAT THE VASSALOVKA FAMILY IS LOSING CONTROL OF THEIR DOMAIN.
VASSALOVKA CRUMBLING?
CAPTAIN SAYS WE'RE WHEELS DOWN IN SEVENTEEN MINUTES, MA'AM.
THANK YOU, LIEUTENANT.
WE NOW GO TO SERÉ COOPER, LIVE IN SAN DIEGO.

OUTRAGE
IN PACIFIC SUB-DOMINION
MORRAY COUNTER ATTACK STRIKES SAN DIEGO.
RELIEF OPERATION UNDERWAY.
LIVE
CEEtv
THANK YOU, JUAN.
SAN DIEGO IS IN RUINS TONIGHT, THE RESULT OF EDGAR MORRAY'S UNPRECEDENTED ATTACK ON A PURELY CIVILIAN TARGET...
...AN ATTACK THAT, IF NOT FOR THE MANDATORY EVACUATION ORDER BY THE FAMILY, COULD HAVE BEEN CATASTROPHIC.
BEET BEET BEET
OPERATION SISYPHUS
DONATE NOW
SAN FRANCISCO
LOS ANGELES
CAMP PENDLETON
YUMA
TUCSON
EL PASO
LUBBOCK
AMARILLO
SERÉ COOPER
SAN DIEGO

GO FOR SANGER.
PRELIMINARY NUMBERS ARE HARD TO COME BY, BUT ESTIMATES PUT SERF DEATHS AT OVER THREE HUNDRED...
UNDER-STOOD.

DAGGER ALPHA IS AT READY ONE AND HAS ACQUIRED THEIR TARGET.
COMMANDER CARLYLE HAS COMMS.
I WANT TO TALK TO HER.
...AMONGST THE WASTE, TEN TIMES THAT NU--

CAN WE HAVE THE ROOM? THANK YOU.
FROM H-O-F, UPLINK COMMS WITH GORGON-ACTUAL.

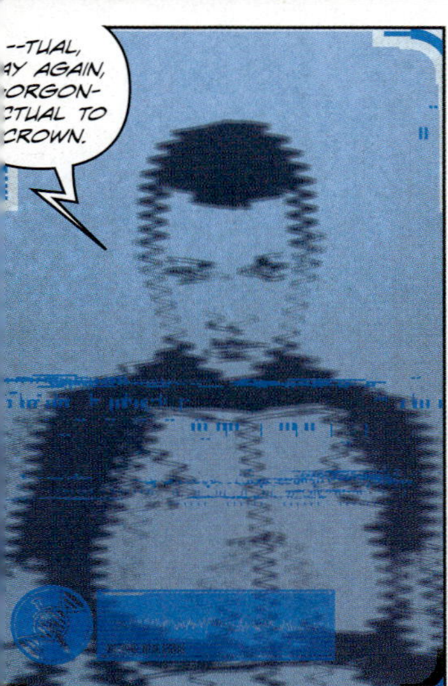
--TUAL, AY AGAIN, ORGON-CTUAL TO CROWN.

I'M HERE, I'M HERE.
YOU'RE IN POSITION? NO PROBLEMS? TELL ME YOU'RE **OKAY.**
I'M FINE, JO, RELAX...
04:59

MILCOMS
...NO PROBLEMS AT ALL. EVERYTHING'S **PREPPED.**
WHERE'RE YOU?

FLYING DOWN TO SAN DIEGO TO INSPECT THE DAMAGE.
SHOULD BE FINISHED ABOUT THE TIME **YOU** ARE--
WAIT! WAIT, FOREVER...
WE HAVE TARGET **INBOUND.** GOT TO GO--

23:59
...JUST...BE **CAREFUL.**
PLEASE.
C'MON, JO, YOU KNOW AS WELL AS I DO...

...CAREFUL WON'T **WIN** THE WAR.

BESIDES...

CARLYLE
ODERINT DUM METUANT

MICHAEL LARK

FRACTURE I

CHAPTER THREE

GINGERSNAP, GORGON. HE'S IN ZONE AND MOVING FAST...

...ESTIMATE TWENTY MINUTES TO CONTACT.
CONFIRM.
LET'S DO THIS.

JORDAN.
COMMANDER?

BY THE NUMBERS, JUST LIKE WE PLANNED.

WOULDN'T DO IT ANY OTHER WAY, MA'AM.

IT IS AS PREDICTED, THEN...

Outside Vladivostok
Family: Vassalovka
Kopylov Territory
...THE DRAGON COMES TO MAKE EXAMPLES OF THOSE WHO WOULD BETRAY VASSALOVKA.
HE COMES, YES, AVTORITET KOPYLOV.

EIGHTEEN MINUTES, GIVE OR TAKE. BUT BEYOND THAT, NOTHING IS CERTAIN.
MHM. YOU HAVE A PLAN.
AND OF MY DAUGHTER? TATIANA?

SHE IS VERY SAFE.
THAT IS WHAT SOMEONE WHO IS KEEPING HER HOSTAGE WOULD SAY.

OR SOMEONE WHO IS TELLING YOU THE TRUTH.

DO YOU KNOW HOW OLD I AM, COMMANDER?
CALL ME FOREVER, PLEASE, SIR.
IF OUR INTELLIGENCE IS TO BE BELIEVED-- AND CONCERNING YOU IT ISN'T--YOU'RE SOMEWHERE IN YOUR LATE EIGHTIES.

YOUR INTELLIGENCE IS NOT FAR OFF. I AM NINETY-THREE, FOREVER.
THE SAME AGE, ROUGHLY, AS YOUR FATHER.
OLD ENOUGH TO REMEMBER THE WORLD BEFORE.

OLD ENOUGH TO NO LONGER CARE ABOUT THIS DAY OR THE NEXT, BUT RATHER THE HUNDRED YEARS TO FOLLOW.

ALSO LIKE YOUR FATHER, PERHAPS?

AH, I SEE...

...HE IS AN OLD FOX, HE DOES NOT SHARE HIS PLANS.
MY SISTER--
OH, YES, YOUR SISTER JOHANNA IS HEAD OF FAMILY, AND CUNNING.

BUT YOUR ATHER IS CARLYLE, ND WHILE HE LIVES HE FAMILY STEERS N HIS DIRECTION, LIKE IT OR NOT.
AND YOU DO NOT KNOW WHERE HE IS TAKING YOU. OR US, FOR THAT MATTER.

AND YOUR OWN DAUGHTER? SHE KNOWS YOUR PLANS?

YES, FOREVER.
SHE MOST CERTAINLY DOES.

BUZZ BUZZ...

...LITTLE BEE...

...HOW I WONDER WHAT YOU SEE.
WEAPONLINK: ACTIVE

HEH.

THWICK

HUH?

TRY--

--HARDER!

THWAK

COWARD
COWARD--

--FOREVER!

GORGON, SPYGLASS. TARGET ELEVEN MINUTES OUT.
GINGERSNAP PUT TWO ON TARGET. NEGATIVE EFFECT.
CONFIRMED. STICK TO THE PLAN.
GORGON OUT.

YOU ARE GOING TO FIND HIM VERY DIFFICULT TO KILL.
AS DIFFICULT AS KILLING YOU. PERHAPS HARDER.
OH, DEFINITELY HARDER.

HEH. YOU HAVE A SENSE OF HUMOR.
THAT IS GOOD...

...KEEPS YOU HUMAN.

WE WERE TALKING ABOUT TATIANA, YES?

...YES.
ABOUT PLANS.
YES, THAT'S RIGHT, MY PLANS FOR HER...

...SHE WILL DESTROY VASSALOVKA.
I'M SURE.
I'M QUITE SERIOUS, FOREVER, I ASSURE YOU.

THEN WHY WERE YOU LOOKING TO ATTACK US? WHY NOT TAKE ON ONE OF YOUR FELLOW AVTORITETS?
OR WAS THE WHOLE THING WITH HOUSE AKLAQ JUST A MISUNDER-STANDING?

SO YOUR SISTER KEEPS YOU AS IN THE DARK AS YOUR FATHER?
I'M NINETY-THREE, FOREVER. I'M GOING TO DIE, SOON.

MY TERRITORY IS BORDERED BY THE BERING SEA TO THE EAST, AVTORITET ZOLOI'S DOMAIN TO THE WEST.
WITH MY PASSING, MY TERRITORY BECOMES TATIANA'S.
AT WHICH POINT ZOLOI INVADES-- WITH VASSALOVKA PERMISSION--CITING HER UNSUITABILITY AS JUSTIFICATION.
UNSUITABILITY?

SHE IS NOT WHITE ENOUGH.

YOU WEREN'T LOOKING TO ANNEX AKLAQ.
YOU WERE LOOKING TO MOVE THERE.

SSSSSS

SSSS
SSSS

NHH

GORGON, BLUE WOLF. FOUR MINUTES.
HAVEN'T DONE MORE THAN PISS HIM **OFF,** HAVE TO SAY.
CONFIRMED. ON MY WAY.

I'M AFRAID I HAVE TO LEAVE YOU NOW, AVTORITET.

YES, YOU DON'T WANT TO BE **LATE.**

AVTORITET KOPYLOV?
YES, FOREVER?

DO **YOU** KNOW WHAT FATHER HAS **PLANNED?**

I'D THINK IT WAS OBVIOUS.
HUMOR ME.

HE WANTS WHAT I WANT, JUST ON A MUCH LARGER SCALE.

YOU WANT TO ENSURE A FUTURE FOR YOUR DAUGHTER.

THAT IS HALF AN ANSWER.
THEN TELL ME THE OTHER HALF.
I DID...

...YOU CLEARLY WEREN'T LISTENING.

GOOD LUCK, COMMANDER CARLYLE.

San Diego,
Pacific Sub-Dominion
Family: Carlyle
...CASUALTY STILL ONGOING, MA'AM.

HOW MANY DEAD?

APPROVED NUMBERS RELEASED FOR DISTRIBUTION VIA THE POST ARE--ESTIMATED--THREE HUNDRED SERF, ROUGHLY THREE THOUSAND WASTE--
NO.

THE REAL NUMBERS.
...I'M... I'M SORRY, MA'AM?

THE REAL NUMBERS. HOW MANY REALLY KILLED?

I, UH...
...THE NUMBERS ON THE SERFS ARE ROUGHLY ACCURATE, MA'AM, THREE HUNDRED SEVENTY-TWO KILLED.

AND?
AND... AND...
...I'M SORRY, MA'AM, I DON'T UNDERSTAND WHAT YOU'RE ASKING?

THE WASTE.
WHAT WERE THE NUMBERS FOR THE WASTE?

I DON'T... WE DON'T NORMALLY...
...I'M AFRAID I DON'T HAVE THAT INFORMA--
HALES

FUCKING. WELL. GET IT.
NOW.

ALL THIS DUST, GETS INTO EVERYTHING, DAMMIT.
MHM.

YOU NEED TO GET ME AN UPGRADE, GET ME THE TWO-TWENTY, IT'S ENCLOSED--
LUIS.
SERÉ?
SHUT UP.

LOOK, YOU MAY NOT CARE RIGHT NOW, BUT IF WE GO LIVE AND THERE'S A SMUDGE ON YOUR PRETTY FACE--

WHAT'S YOUR ZOOM LIKE?

WITHOUT THE DIGITAL AUGMENT? OR WITH?
LUIS.
FIFTEEN BY, CAN GET IT UP TO FIFTY. WHY?

OH.
RACK HER UP, I WANT TO SEE WHAT'S GOING ON.

SERÉ! THAT'S HEAD OF FAMILY!
WE DON'T FILM HEAD OF FAMILY WITHOUT PERMISSION!
I JUST WANT TO SEE WHAT'S GOING ON, LUIS...

...THAT'S NOT FILMING, THAT'S JUST LOOKING.

THIS IS A BAD IDEA.
DON'T BE SUCH A FUCKING BABY, LUIS.
FOCUS ON JOHANNA...

...I WANT TO SEE HER EXPRESSION, I CAN'T TELL WHAT'S GOING ON...
ZOOM 1X

ZOOM 3X

ZOOM 5X

ZOOM 7X

ZOOM 12X

GORGON-ACTUAL, ALL TEAMS.
TARGET ON SITE, REPEAT, TARGET IS **ON SITE.**

--SPYGLASS, GINGERSNAP, WHAT'S THE **SHOT?**
NO SHOT, **REPEAT,** NO SHOT...

...BANSHEE, GORGON-ACTUAL, ON COUNTDOWN.
TELL ME LONGSWORD IS IN POSITION, SOMEONE--

PLAYING GAMES

--WE'RE FUCKED IF--
LONGSWORD, I AM HERE.

KOPYLOV!
TRAITOR!

IN POSITION.
GORGON-ACTUAL, LONGSWORD, STAND BY.

...STAND BY...
HAVE IT YOUR WAY
KRRSHH
KRRSHH
MEET
YOUR
END

HNNGH

JESUS FUCK, HOW IS HE STILL ALIVE?

NHN

MOVING TO ENGAGE.
DAGGER ALPHA, ON MY ORDER...

EARS

...NOW.

HURTS

FUNNY.
HE WAS SO MUCH MORE IMPRESSIVE, LAST TIME.
SONJA, BE NICE...

...THE POOR THING CAN HARDLY HELP HOW HE WAS MADE.
KILL--

--YOU!
I'M THIRSTY. YOU THIRSTY?

I AM, RATHER.
WHAT

SO, HOW'VE YOU BEEN?
OH, YOU KNOW, BUSY...
YOU CAN'T

YOU DON'T GET TO WALK AWAY!

SURE WE DO.

NNHHHH

HHHHH

HHAAAA

AAAAAA

AAAKILL--

--YOUKILL--

--YOU

...OPERATION WAS SUCCESSFUL?

WE ACHIEVED OUR DESIRED OBJECTIVE, YES, SIR.
INTERESTING.
THEN YOU NEVER INTENDED TO TRY TO KILL HIM.

NO, SIR, WE DID NOT.
WISE.
THIS IS YOUR SECOND ENGAGEMENT WIT THE ZMEY, I BELIEV COMMANDER. YOU LEARN QUICKLY.

MISS BITTNER, I HAVE NOT HAD THE PLEASURE.
AVTORITET VLADISLOV MIKHAILOVICH, THE PLEASURE IS MINE.

AND SO VERY POLITE.
NOW WHAT HAPPENS?

E'RE HEADING
O VANCOUVER.
R DAUGHTER
AWAITS YOU
THERE.
I HAVE NO INTENTION OF ABANDONING MY LANDS, COMMANDER.

NOR DO WE.

HMM.
A GUERILLA WAR, THEN? YOUR FAMOUS DAGGERS AS, HOW DO YOU SAY, ADVISORS?

SOMETHING LIKE THAT.
VERY WELL. I CONSENT, EVEN THOUGH IT IS CLEAR SUCH IS NOT REQUIRED.

YOU AND YOUR SISTER ARE PLAYING A BOLD GAME, COMMANDER. BOLDER, PERHAPS, THAN OLD MEN SUCH AS YOUR FATHER AND I CAN STILL STOMACH.
LET US HOPE THE PRICE IS NOT TOO HIGH.

PRICE, AS MEN LIKE YOU AND HE HAVE TAUGHT US, AVTORITET, IS NO OBJECT.

Southern Sierra Nevadas
Facility: Compound Sequoia
Family: Carlyle

COPY AND ENCRYPT.
DOWNLOAD TO MOBILE.
DA-DEEP

TRANSPORT.
DWEET
ELLISON. WHAT CAN I DO FOR YOU, DOCTOR CARLYLE?

I'M HEADED TO CENTER.
WE'LL GET HER FUELED AND READY, DOCTOR.

THANK YOU, LIEUTENANT.

DING DING

DING DING

DING DING
COME.

SORRY TO INTERRUPT.

AREN'T YOU SUPPOSED TO BE DOING EIGHT'S BI-WEEKLY?
MARISOL TOOK HER OUT FOR SOME WILDERNESS TRAINING.

THAT WASN'T SCHEDULED.

I THINK IT WAS SUPPOSED TO BE A SURPRISE.
FOR HER OR ME?

SHE FUCKING SHOULD'VE SCHEDULED IT WITH ME.
GIVE IT HERE.

THIS THE TELEMETRY FROM THE MORRAY-D'SOUZA ENGAGEMENT?
YES.

LOOKS GOOD.
IT IS GOOD. SHE'S RUNNING TWENTY PERCENT ABOVE PROJECTIONS.
I MEAN, IT'S BETTER THAN GOOD, IT'S AMAZING...

...FOREVER'S NEVER BEEN BETTER.
IF THERE'S A "BUT" IN THAT SENTENCE, JAMES, FUCKING WELL SAY IT.

...BUT I FOUND AN ANOMALY WITH THE TELEMETRY ITSELF.
ANOMALY HOW?
PACKET DEGRADATION.
MEANING?

I THINK SOMEONE'S GHOSTING HER TELEMETRY.

MOTHER FUCK.
ARE YOU CERTAIN?

THERE COULD BE OTHER--
NO! NOT GOOD ENOUGH, JAMES!

BE CERTAIN.
BE ABSOLUTELY CERTAIN...

...AND BE ABSOLUTELY CERTAIN BY THE TIME I GET BACK.

RAFFETTO.
IT'S MARISOL.
HEY, GUNNY. I JUST WENT OFF-SHIFT. I'LL PATCH YOU THROUGH TO THE DUTY OFFICER IF--
NO, I'M TALKING TO YOU DIRECT, JIMMY...

...I NEED A FAVOR.
OUTSIDE CHANNELS.

...
WHAT DO YOU NEED?

Puget Sound
Facility: The Center
Family: Carlyle

TIME
A GREAT
EACHER...

...BUT UNFORTUNATELY IT KILLS ALL ITS STUDENTS.
HECTOR BERLIOZ.

ALL THESE YEARS, I THOUGHT IT WOULD BE **ME** COMING TO YOU, FINALLY WEARING YOU **DOWN.**
BUT THAT WAS **NEVER** WHAT YOU WERE WAITING FOR, WAS IT?
NO, MALCOLM...

...I WAS WAITING FOR YOU TO **DIE.**

WELL, YOU'VE GOT WHAT YOU WERE WAITING FOR, ABBY.
BETHANY JUST LEFT.

I KNOW.
I'M SURE SHE BLAMES HERSELF.
SHE ALWAYS DID.
YOU SHOULD TALK TO HER.

SHE COULD USE HER MOTHER RIGHT NOW.
WOULD YOU SHARE A DRINK WITH ME? FOR WHAT WE WERE, IF NOT WHAT WE ARE?

GOOD NIGHT, MALCOLM.

I DON'T WANT TO G BACK.

I KNOW.
BUT THAT'S NOT AN OPTION, EVE.

WE STAY OUT HERE MUCH LONGER, THEY'LL COME LOOKING.
AND THERE'LL BE QUESTIONS...

...WE HAVE TO GO BACK.
I KNOW--

--WAIT--
SHHH!
WH--

CAN'T YOU **HEAR** IT?

SOMEONE'S **COMING.**

JO?

JO!

WHOA! EASY!
I DIDN'T-- I DIDN'T THINK IT WAS **YOU,** I DIDN'T THINK--
--I THOUGHT YOU WERE WORKING--

--I DIDN'T THINK YOU...
...I'M IN **TROUBLE.** AM I IN **TROUBLE?**

OH, KIDDO. **NO,** NO YOU'RE **NOT.**
AT LEAST NOT HOW YOU **THINK.**

THERE'S SOMEONE I WANT YOU TO **MEET.**

HELLO, FOREVER.
I'VE BEEN...
...I'M VERY **HAPPY** TO FINALLY MEET YOU.
I'M YOUR **SISTER,** YOUR **OTHER** SISTER.
MY NAME'S **FOREVER...**

...JUST LIKE **YOU...**

CARLYLE
ODERINT DUM METUANT

Page 145: Michael Lark's unused coloring scheme for the cover of *Lazarus: Risen* #2. After much deliberation, the darker, more apocalyptic reds and oranges of the final cover were wedded to Trautmann's designs for Joacquim Morray's "point of view" computer systems.
(Art: **Michael Lark**.)

Page 146: House Aklaq controls much of the northern portion of Carlyle territory. As the war rages on, Vassalovka flexes its muscles and has made inroads to Carlyle's north. Note the graffiti, featuring a stylized Vassalovka "V" insignia, and the ominous Cyrillic notation "We are coming."
(Artifact: **Richard Howe.** Text: **Eric Trautmann**.)

Page 147: With the growing global conflict, Carlyle's media and propaganda apparatus—notably through the omnipresent Post and CEEtv programming—must remain nimble. Even marketing posters for popular action-adventure programming like *Strikeforce Echo* have to be carefully directed. In this case, the show's ongoing storyline has pivoted to Morray's actual betrayal.
(Artifact and text: **Eric Trautmann**.)

Page 148: Vassalovka spies could lurk around every corner, citizens of Carlyle! Carlyle Navy (CARNAV) propaganda poster.
(Artifact: **Richard Howe.** Text: **Eric Trautmann**.)

Page 149: In reaction to Morray's counterstrike into Carlyle territory, CEEtv and the cast of the popular situation comedy *Guns Up!* host a benefit for those injured and displaced by the attacks.
(Artifact: **Richard Howe.** Text: **Eric Trautmann**.)

Page 150: Think of the children! CEEtv public service announcement.
(Artifact: **Richard Howe.** Text: **Eric Trautmann**.)

Page 151: Poster for Anti-Vassalovka propaganda film, *Matryoshka*. Evil Vassalovka terror scientists have developed a horrifying bioweapon, converting viable fetuses into scores of ravenous creatures devouring their mothers from within. The popular star of *Guns Up!* hoped this would be his big dramatic break, but this was not to be.
(Artifact and text: **Richard Howe**.)

RE ENTERING TERRITORY CONTROL
OUSE AK AQ
CARLYLE
МЫ!
ИДЁМ
INSTRUCTIONS
AKLAQ TERRITORIAL MA AGEM NT BY AU OF FAMILY CARLYLE.
ALL CARLYLE REGULATIONS, RULES, AND

Adjust color/ lighting

More "noon-day" hue

DOWN. NEVER OUT.

Delete

Morray made it personal.
Now Echo gets even.

All Caps

STRIKEFORCE ECHO

SUBSCRIBE VIA POST @STRIKEFORCE_SEASON7

GOLD & PLATINUM TIER ACCOUNTS VISIT POST_BTS_SFE FOR BEHIND-THE-SCENES FOOTAGE

CEEtv

CEETV_PROMO_V8.1_STRIKEFORCE ECHO S7_RC1

DIRECTIVE

Office of Head of Family
CENTER, Cascadia Sub-dominion

15 FEB 67
cc: Head of Family
Media Oversight Board
CEEtv General Management
CEEtv Original Content Group
CEEtv Strikeforce Echo Production Staff

Stanley (and team):

We've received your first round of comps for the new "Strikeforce Echo" print campaign for season 7. Upon review, Jo C. and I have some concerns, which I'm sure you'll rectify immediately.

"Strikeforce Echo" is, as you know, first and foremost intended to reinforce the viewer's perception of the skill and determination of CARSEC/Int groups, particularly during the current state of real-world hostility we are engaged in. Jo particularly wants you to de-emphasize negative outcomes for Carlyle. (For example, remove "Down" from the current promotional tagline. Setbacks are necessary for drama, of course, but let's not harp on it in our publicity material, okay?) "Never out" is a perfect summation of this concept, however. Develop similar taglines for review.

Also, emphasize the elements of retribution and revenge. (Example: All-caps in "Echo gets EVEN.")

Overall color schemes should be brighter. The drama of more apocalyptic themes is compelling, but focus instead on themes of Carlyle grit as the thin line between order and chaos.

Resubmit with changes by tomorrow, 0900.

BEWARE
OF VASSALOVKA SPIES

NEW WAR. SAME OLD TRICKS.

They seem nice, don't they? The smiling barista who hands you your morning coffee. The kind man who helps you with your groceries. The new neighbor, just trying to make a friend.

Or perhaps they'll take a different approach, offering to fulfill your darkest, wildest **FANTASIES**.

Don't be fooled. **AGENTS** are being employed by our foes, intent on securing intelligence from unwary **CARNAV** personnel.

BE ON GUARD against prying questions or overly inquisitive strangers. Remember: if it seems too good to be true, **IT IS**.

Treat **EVERYTHING** as secret. Report any inquiries from outside the chain of command as **ESPIONAGE**.

See **ALL**.

Say **NOTHING**.

SILENCE IS SECURITY.

MALWARE INTRUSION HUB

TRANQ CAPSULES

GARROTE

NETWORK DISRUPTER

SPYWARE DRIVE

CONCEALED MICRODRONE

Report suspicious activity to **CARNAV INTERNAL SECURITY** immediately via **POST.MIL.HONEYTRAPHOTLINE@spywatch.7.mi**

MICHAEL **ANASTASIA** · CON **CASPERBECK** · JENNIFER **BRAZIUNOS** · FRANK **FULLMAN** · MITT **TOLBERT** · FIONA **McCALL** · AND HUGO **RAGE**

GUNS UP!

FOR THE RELOCATED

Join the cast of the top-rated show for a special evening to benefit the Carlyle citizens temporarily displaced by OPERATION: SISYPHUS and its aftermath.

Featuring

LIVE PERFORMANCES OF FAN-FAVORITE EPISODES

THERE'S SOMETHING ABOUT SARGE
The one that started it all!

THE DURANGO DILEMMA
The platoon takes on Morray for a taste of the "good stuff"!

DRAWN DOWN
The animated classic—performed live!

Directed by Series Creator Hermés Ericksson

SATURDAY
APRIL 13

STANDARD ACCESS TIER: ©150
GOLD ACCESS TIER: ©1,800
PLATINUM ACCESS TIER: ©2,200

THE GRACE
7:30 PM

LIVESTREAM VIA POST AT COMEDY/GUNSUP/BENEFIT@POST.ENTERTAINMENT

Donation Coordinators on site. Bring any non-perishable food items, clothing, and first aid supplies. LRP Donations accepted.

THE ABIGAIL FOUNDATION

WHAT DOES SHE SEE?

CEEtv is proud to provide quality content to all, from upper-tier subscription programming to free educational and entertainment titles distributed via The Post.

But one size does not fit all. In these challenging times, it is vital to ensure that younger viewers are not exposed to inappropriate material. Parental Content Monitoring and Restriction Tools are available to subscribers through your system profile menu.

Safety and security is our top priority. For our family. For your family. For *all* families.

Households with children 13 and under should enable Parental Content Monitoring today.

9812.182

Some features are not available to all subscri
Public/free accounts may be assessed fees for activating content t

EVIL COMES
FROM WITHIN

TOO DARK!
ARE YOU PEOPLE HIGH?

Match
VFX
Better!!

Find
Better Doll—
TOO CUTE

LOOKS KIND
OF FAKE

FROM THE PRODUCERS OF BLOOD OF THE DRAGON

CON CASPERBECK ALISON POPPY

MATRYOSHKA

CEEtv IN ASSOCIATION WITH FAMILY FILMS PRESENTS A BETTER THAN ONE PRODUCTION A PETER BENJAMIN FILM "MATRYOSHKA" ALISON POPPY
WITH MOLLY DUETT MATT YUGUCHI FLORA GALLEGO AND INTRODUCING DASHIELL NATASCHA ROB HERMANN ROB PAWSON RICHARD GARFINKEL THOMAS PENNINGTON
MARTIN BROPHY ANDREW BAUTOVICH NATHAN AGIUS EVIENNE ZANDER AND CHELSEA BONSKER HERMÈS ERICKSSON & DAVID KURTZ
17+ DAVID KURTZ FEBRUARY 21 PETER BENJAMIN

Matryoshka_KA_R26_C754

Vaughn—
Great job, as usual.
ome bad news, though...
r studies of test audience
back show resistance to Con
ramatic part, so they're
tting him out of it.
, they're only paying
inimal re-shoots.
names above title, and
of golden boy.
this to yourself.
told Con yet.

CARLYLE
ODERINT DUM METUANT